STRETCHY
LESSON PLANS

Pat Miller

Fort Atkinson, Wisconsin

Dedicated to Mary Stevenson Gallagher
St. Ed's Roommate and Educator Extraordinaire

Credits

Pages 34–38: *George Washington's Teeth* tag game adapted from Suzy Red's game with permission (www.suzyred.com/2004washington.html).

Pages 42–43: "100 Cool Teachers in Children's Literature" list reprinted with permission from "A Year of Reading: Two Teachers Who Read. A Lot." — the blog of Franki and Mary Lee.

Pages 46–49: Substitute Groundhog Readers' Theater Script reprinted with permission from *LibrarySparks* Volume 4, Issue 6.

Published by UpstartBooks
W5527 State Road 106
P.O. Box 800
Fort Atkinson, Wisconsin 53538-0800
1-800-448-4887

Contents

Works for Me!

Useful Tips

Reminder

 Humor

Additional Lessons

Introduction

I was inspired to write this book by a woman at a library conference. After one of my presentations, we visited and she said, "I wish I could be a fly on the wall of your library—a fly with a notebook!" This series is for her, and for others who wonder what I do with my students "in the real world." It's also a good way for me to meet my annual resolution to get my lessons more organized!

If you're like me, you want to know how similar my situation is to yours. I'm a library media specialist in a suburban school of 940 students with a full-time aide. Our population is becoming more diverse, and we are adding more ELL classes from PreK through fifth grade. This is my nineteenth year as a librarian, preceded by 15 years as a classroom teacher. I've been a librarian at four schools in diverse situations.

I've been the only librarian for more than 1,200 elementary students (ten classes in most grades), and at a smaller school where many of my students' families were on welfare. I've been "in the rotation" when I taught classes to give the teachers their planning time. I've worked for avid library supporters and one who just wanted me to keep the kids quiet and the parents out of his office. I've worked without an aide, with an aide, and with a cadre of talented mother volunteers.

My current schedule is to see every child every week for check out, but to teach a fixed lesson to intermediates one week, and to their primary partners the next. In a typical month, that means only two lessons per grade. This is a Stretchy Lesson Plan book because I've included more lessons than one would use in a month. The lessons can stretch to fit a number of grade levels and will last for years without repeating if you have my kind of schedule. And best of all, the lessons are bound to trigger some great ideas of your own.

Do I Need These If I Have the Stretchy Library Lessons Books?

The SLL books are invaluable books of lessons for library skills, reading and reference activities, and multicultural and seasonal celebrations. One never has too many lessons from which to choose the best fit for his or her students. One difference is that this series is designed to give you not just lessons, but useful tips, forms, strategies, and reminders that I have developed or discovered over the years. This book is also an organizational tool, correlating additional ideas from the six books of the Stretchy Library Lessons series, the six Collaborative Bridges books, and the first 36 issues of *LibrarySparks*. Add these to your favorite lessons, adapting them to your own students.

Because the lessons from my other books are ones that I often use, those will be referenced in each book. You will have a list of six to eight additional lessons each month from my other books, as well as articles from the first four years of *LibrarySparks* magazine. I write these books not only for you, but also for myself, and I needed a resource that had all those things in one place for easy reference.

In this series, in one place, you have additional lessons for each month, along with useful tips, calendar correlations, forms, patterns, lots of books, and inspiration for your own planning. Whether you wonder how to find a lesson plan form that fits your schedule, how to run a successful book fair, or how to find good literature each week, the answers are here. This is not the definitive plan book, but it will guide you through the year, your library curriculum, and the special events that make your program more fun for students.

How to Use This Book

If you teach in the library, this book is for you. It will help you if you are a certified librarian with a master's degree and extensive experience or if you are a novice librarian in your first elementary library. I hope it will be especially helpful if you are an uncertified aide or generous volunteer. My hat is off to all of you who are constantly looking for ways to meet the needs of your students.

Lessons featured in this book represent many of the lessons I actually have used through the years. Sometimes teachable moments, special events, or collaborative units will bump lessons off your schedule, but these will give you a good start. Each book will include four lessons for grades K–2 and four for grades 3–5. I've also included a number of tips about how I do things in my library that seem to make life easier for my students and me, and might work for you as well.

Each lesson includes:

- **Objective(s):** Why teach this lesson? What student need will it address? How does it correlate to the curriculum?

- **Grades:** This indicates whether the lesson is intended for primary grades or intermediate grades. However, I'm confident that if you are using this book, you are also the person who can adapt any lesson and thrive in any situation.

- **Materials:** These are readily available or easily made and should be gathered before you teach the lesson.

- **Prepare in Advance:** If you teach all grades each day as I do, your lesson materials need to be well organized because there is little time between classes. This section tells you what needs to be made, purchased, or found before your class comes in.

- **Activity Directions:** My schedule is fixed at 45-minute classes, with a few bands of flexible time that can be scheduled by any teacher. The following lessons are designed for approximately 30 minutes and include all forms, worksheets, and patterns that you will need.

- **Resources:** This section lists books to use in place of the featured book or as companion books to it. Use them in a display, share them with teachers or plan extension lessons with them. Web sites are included here and can often be the basis for additional lessons. As I write, the books are in print and the Web sites are current. If you get an error message when using the address, perform a keyword search on the site title. If a book is out of print, check www.amazon.com.

What's Happening This Month?

February is the short month that relieves the doldrums of January with President's Day, Valentine's Day, Groundhog Day, and Mardi Gras. We celebrate Black History Month, Dental Health Month, Library Lover's Month, and National Bird Feeding Month.

Set up a birthday display with "Thanks, (author name), for the presents!" Display a fake birthday cake and attach birthday streamers, party hats, etc. If you don't have a handy bulletin board, use a science fair display board. Attach author pictures if you have them from Internet sites, publisher flyers, or book jackets. Then add the birthday books and encourage check out.

Look for 12 pages of Birthday Celebration ideas in *Stretchy Library Lessons: Seasons and Celebrations.* In your birthday display, you can feature the books by these authors:

Author Birthdays			
Langston Hughes	Feb. 1	David Small	Feb. 12
Jerry Spinelli	Feb. 1	Jacqueline Woodson	Feb. 12
Judith Viorst	Feb. 2	Janet Taylor Lisle	Feb. 13
Joan Lowery Nixon	Feb. 3	William Sleator	Feb. 13
Russell Hoban	Feb. 4	Simms Taback	Feb. 13
Patricia Lauber	Feb. 5	George Shannon	Feb. 14
David Wiesner	Feb. 5	Paul Zelinsky	Feb. 14
Betsy Duffey	Feb. 6	Norman Bridwell	Feb. 15
Laura Ingalls Wilder	Feb. 7	Robert Newton Peck	Feb. 17
Anne Rockwell	Feb. 8	Mary Blount Christian	Feb. 20
Dick Gackenbach	Feb. 9	Jim Aylesworth	Feb. 21
Stephen Gammell	Feb. 10	C. S. Adler	Feb. 23
E. L. Konigsburg	Feb. 10	Walter Wick	Feb. 23
Mark Teague	Feb. 10	Cynthia Voigt	Feb. 25
Jane Yolen	Feb. 11	Donna Jo Napoli	Feb. 28
Judy Blume	Feb. 12		

Meet these authors in the pages of *LibrarySparks* magazine:

Catherine Stock (illustrator) 2007 (K–2, 3–5)

Christopher Myers (illustrator) 2007 (K–2, 3–5)

Christopher Paul Curtis 2004 (3–5)

Deborah Wiles 2007 (3–5)

Ed Young 2006 (K–2, 3–5)

Eric Kimmel 2005 (K–2, 3–5)

Kelly DiPucchio 2006 (K–2)

National Bird Feeding Month

- Make a simple pinecone feeder at Mister Rogers's Web site: pbskids.org/rogers/R_house/object19.htm.

- *About Birds: A Guide for Children* by Cathryn Sill. Peachtree Publishers, 1991.

- *Backyard Birding for Kids: A Field Guide & Activities* by Fran Lee. Gibbs Smith, 2005.

- *Backyard Birds* by Jonathan P. Latimer and Karen Stray Nolting. Houghton Mifflin, 1999.

- *Backyard Pets: Activities for Exploring Wildlife Close to Home* by Carol A. Amato. Jossey-Bass, 2002.

- *Bird Watcher* by David Burnie. DK, 2005.

- *Feathered Friends of Texas: A Birdwatching Guide for Children* by Jane Scoggins Bauld. Eakin Press, 2004.

- *Feeding Our Feathered Friends* by Dean T. Spaulding. Lerner Publishing Group, 1997.

- *Take a Backyard Bird Walk* by Jane Kirkland, Dorothy Burke, and Melanie Palaisa. Stillwater Publishing, 2004.

Biographies of two birders who loved and studied "backyard birds"

- *Birds in the Bushes: A Story about Margaret Morse Nice* by Julie Dunlap. Carolrhoda Books, 1996.

- *The Boy Who Drew Birds: A Story of John James Audubon* by Jacqueline Davies. Houghton Mifflin, 2004.

- *Into the Woods: John James Audubon Lives His Dream* by Robert Burleigh. Atheneum Books for Young Readers, 2003.

Black History Month

In addition to new biographies on outstanding African Americans, feature these nonfiction titles:

- *The Buffalo Soldier* by Sherry Garland. Pelican Publishing, 2006.

- *The Escape of Oney Judge: Martha Washington's Slave Finds Freedom* by Emily Arnold McCully. Farrar, Straus and Giroux, 2007.

- *George Crum and the Saratoga Chip* by Gaylia Taylor. Lee & Low Books, 2006.

- *The Harlem Hellfighters: When Pride Met Courage* by Walter Dean Myers and Bill Miles. HarperCollins, 2006.

- *Jesse Owens: Fastest Man Alive* by Carole Boston Weatherford. Walker & Co., 2007.

- *Vision of Beauty: The Story of Sarah Breedlove Walker* by Kathryn Lasky. Candlewick Press, 2003.

These fiction books present an interesting viewpoint.

- *Away West* by Patricia C. McKissack. Viking, 2006.

- *Porch Lies: Tales of Slicksters, Tricksters, and Other Wily Characters* by Patricia C. McKissack. Schwartz & Wade Books, 2006. Short stories that can be shared and enjoyed in a library period.

- *Sienna's Scrapbook: Our African-American Heritage Trip* by Toni Trent Parker. Chronicle Books, 2005.

- *Stealing Home* by Ellen Schwartz. Tundra Books, 2006.

Make crafts to help celebrate Black History Month.

African-American Crafts Kids Can Do! by Carol Gnojewski. Enslow Publishers, Inc., 2006.

Crafts That Celebrate Black History by Kathy Ross. Millbrook Press, 2002.

Dental Health Month

- *Andrew's Loose Tooth* by Robert Munsch. Scholastic, 2002.

- *Brush Well: A Look at Dental Care* by Katie Bagley. Bridgestone Books, 2002.

- *A Day in the Life of a Dentist* by Heather Adamson. Capstone Press, 2004.

- Dental Health series for primary grades by Helen Frost (Pebble Books), including *Brushing Well, Food for Healthy Teeth, Going to the Dentist,* and *Your Teeth.*

- *Dental Hygienists* by Fran Hodgkins. Bridgestone Books, 2001.

- *Dentist* by Jacqueline Laks Gorman.Weekly Reader Early Learning Library, 2002.

- *Just Going to the Dentist* by Mercer Mayer. Golden Books, 2003.

- *My Mouth* by Lloyd G. Douglas. Children's Press, 2004.

- *Open Wide: Tooth School Inside* by Laurie Keller. Henry Holt & Company, 2003.

- *Staying Healthy* by Angela Royston. Raintree, 2004.

- *Teeth* by Beth Ferguson. Benchmark Books, 2004.

- *Vera Goes to the Dentist* by Vera Rosenberry. Henry Holt & Company, 2002.

Library Lovers' Month (See list of books about books and reading on pages 42–43.)

February Library Events
February School Events

Healthy Foods

Objectives: To learn the names of healthy foods from the vegetable group. To learn how natural remedies are still used today. To become familiar with paper engineering.

Grades: K–2

Materials:

- a globe or world map

- fresh ginger root (in the vegetable section of the supermarket)

- a bottle of ginger ale

- ginger snaps

- a vegetable peeler

- a book about gingerbread (see resource list)

- gingerbread character (optional)

Principal Observation

Since it was my first school and my first book fair I invited my mother to stop by. When she arrived I introduced my mother to the second grade teacher watching her class as they looked at the books. Now this class was rather lively and I noticed that they were very subdued as they looked at books.

Later that evening my mother commented on how well behaved the second graders were. When I commented that they were very quiet and not like their usual selves, my mother told me that she overheard two of the students talking. One second grade student told a classmate, "Ms. Taylor must be in trouble if her mother had to come to school to see the principal!"

—Ms. Andre Taylor, Librarian
Houston Elementary School, Washington DC

- vegetables—use pictures or flannel, fun foam, or papier-mâché versions in a large basket

- I introduced this lesson by making Kimberly Faurot's "Story Soup," (see *LibrarySparks,* November 2004, pp. 37–43). If you want to do the same, gather the materials she lists.

- books by Robert Sabuda, including *Cookie Count,* or other book containing gingerbread (see resource list)

Prepare in Advance:

1. Purchase and gather materials. When shopping for ginger snaps, check ingredients carefully. Many have no ginger at all. I found one brand of ginger snaps contained red pepper and chili powder. Look to see if the package warns that the product was prepared in a factory that also processes nut products in case you have nut allergies.

2. Assemble ingredients near story area. When I adapted Kimberly's "Story Soup," I hid a stuffed gingerbread character under a shiny blue piece of material we were using as the water before the activity started. I spelled out "Story Soup" on a cookie sheet using magnetic letters and used 4x4" pieces of paper, several pictures, and a small book cover. Set up a globe to show where China is.

3. Place the ginger snaps in a resealable container. Provide a trash can nearby for students who dislike the taste to dispose of the cookies.

4. I used the vegetable peeler to expose a new section of the ginger for each class to smell. The ginger piece I had was about 8 x 10" so students could really see what a strange looking thing fresh ginger is.

Activity Directions:

1. Either make Story Soup according to the instructions in the magazine or have the students choose a vegetable from the basket to show and name for the class.

2. Tell students that not only are parts of vegetables plants healthy for their bodies overall, but some plant parts are actually useful as remedies and medicines. Show students the ginger. It is often called ginger root, but is actually a rhizome—a thick underground stem. It can be eaten fresh (shaved on a cheese grater for example) or dried as a spice. Ginger can also be used as a medicine and has been in China and other eastern countries for thousands of years (show on the globe).

3. Show them a piece of ginger with the skin peeled off. It is a pale yellow color. Then show them a bottle of ginger ale and ask if anyone has ever had it. Do they remember when they last drank some? Was it because they were sick? Every class I've used this lesson with has had students who report they drank it when they had an upset stomach. Pour some into a glass if desired to show them the yellow color. Tell them that ginger is a word sometimes used to describe a color that is a brownish yellow, like a ginger cat or ginger hair.

4. Ginger is also used as a spice in cake (called gingerbread) and cookies (ginger snaps). Today we are going to share an unusual book about cookies that has an entire gingerbread house inside! (Vary this step to suit the book you choose to share.)

5. Use background information from Robert Sabuda's Web site (www.robertsabuda.com) to explain to children about his work as a paper engineer. Show them the pages of *Cookie Count,* and let them marvel at how the parts spin and crunch and jump up from the page. Sabuda said that what's even harder than engineering illustrations to pop up from the page is engineering them to fold back down without becoming squashed! That's why he has a very large trash can in his art studio.

6. As students prepare to leave, tell them you are going to give them a ginger snap if they are brave enough to try it. I tell them they need to know the three S's of getting the most from a ginger snap. The first is to snap it—show them how to break it with their two thumbs held side by side on the top. Second is to sniff the broken edges—ginger! The third? Snarf it up! Suggest they take a small bite first to see if they like it. Discard if they don't—eat it all up if they do.

Resources:

Selected pop-up books by Robert Sabuda:

Alice's Adventures in Wonderland. Simon & Schuster, 2003.

Cookie Count: A Tasty Pop-Up. Simon & Schuster, 1997.

The Movable Mother Goose. Simon & Schuster, 1999.

The Wonderful Wizard of Oz. Simon & Schuster, 2000.

Selected books by Robert Sabuda and Matthew Reinhart:

Encyclopedia Prehistorica: Dinosaurs. Candlewick Press, 2005.

Encyclopedia Prehistorica: Sharks & Sea Monsters. Candlewick Press, 2006.

Pop-Up Handbook: Butterflies. Hyperion, 2001.

Non-traditional Gingerbread Man books:

The Fairytale Cake by Mark Sperring. Scholastic, 2005.

Gingerbread Baby by Jan Brett. Putnam, 1999.

Ginger Bear by Mini Grey. Knopf, 2007.

The Gingerbread Boy by Richard Egielski. Laura Geringer Books, 1997.

The Gingerbread Cowboy by Janet Squires. Laura Geringer Books, 2006.

The Gingerbread Girl by Lisa Campbell Ernst. Dutton Children's Books, 2006.

The Gingerbread Kid Goes to School by Joan Holub. Grosset & Dunlap, 2002.

The Gingerbread Rabbit by Randall Jarrell. HarperCollins, 2003.

The Jalapeno Man by Debbie Leland. Wildflower Run Publications, 2000.

The Truth About Hansel and Gretel by Karina Law. Picture Window Books, 2005.

Extension: You might want to reproduce the recipe below to share with teachers. History records ginger's medicinal use for more than 2,000 years.

General Robert E. Lee's Ginger Snaps

During the Civil War, both sides used durable ginger snaps to help soldiers recover from nausea and stomach and intestinal upsets, and to ward off colds.

- 3/4 lb. butter, melted
- 1/2 c. molasses
- 2 c. sugar
- 2 eggs
- 4–5 c. flour

- 4 tsp. baking soda
- 2 tsp. cinnamon
- 1 tsp. ginger
- 1 tsp. cloves

Beat together butter, molasses, sugar, and eggs. Add 4 cups flour, soda, cinnamon, ginger, and cloves. Refrigerate mixture for 2 hours. Work in additional flour if necessary. Shape into small balls (1") and roll in sugar. Bake at 350 degrees for 8 to 10 minutes. Makes 10 dozen.

Introducing and Circulating Audio Books

I had purchased a number of audio books that I wanted to introduce to students. The best way to promote them is for students to hear them, so I selected 10 of them that represented nonfiction, realistic fiction, historical fiction, and fantasy. Before we began, we reviewed the reproducible included on page 25. I constantly stress that Fiction is "From Imagination"—I don't accept "fake," "make-believe," "not real," or other definitions. They confuse students when you start talking about realistic fiction.

Students numbered their papers to 10. I told them the title of the book, showed the cover, then had them listen to the first line or first paragraphs of the audio book. Hearing the different voices and the variety of beginnings really stirred interest in the audio books and the print versions as well. John Erickson's audio versions of his Hank the Cowdog series caused a run on his books.

Because this is a new media in our library and the collection is limited, we began with fifth graders only and then added fourth after six weeks. We plan to add third graders when our collection grows. My goal in using audio books is to encourage and involve the passive and reluctant readers, especially boys. The PlayAways (books on a player that resembles an I-Pod) were a huge hit.

The audio books and PlayAways range from $25 to $50 each. Before students can check one out, they have to bring in a signed permission form and two AAA batteries. We hope that gives us enough batteries—along with the ones that came with the PlayAways and the ones the library can provide—to get through the year.

The permission form we use is on page 14. Other considerations are these:

- We shelve the media together rather than inter-shelve it with the books so students can more readily find them. An advantage of shelving them with the books would be to keep them next to their print copy for children to select and read along.

- The books on CD contain all their disks while they are on the shelf. The PlayAway boxes are empty. When a child checks out the box, the PlayAway unit is put into the box at the circulation desk along with an extra battery.

- We have parent volunteers who help with circulation. However, all audio books are put into a labeled box when they are returned for my aide to check over carefully. She is the one who charges for damages or loss, so she will be able to vouch that a CD or PlayAway was in good shape when each user takes it.

- We added a neon orange label inside the PlayAway box that states "Be sure the unit is off after each use."

- Students can only have one audio book checked out at a time.

- To identify which students have permission to check out audio books, we put a gold happy face sticker on their library card.

Audio Books Permission Slip

I give my permission for my child, _____ ,

to check out audio books from the library.

The books are in DVD format and PlayAway format (looks like an MP3 player).
I understand that:

(Please initial each)

_____ This program is currently only for fourth and fifth grade due to limited materials (fourth grade will begin in the third six weeks).

_____ If my child damages or loses an audiobook, I will pay the replacement value which ranges from $25.00 to $50.00.

_____ Materials will be checked out for two weeks. They can only be renewed once, due to high demand. I will help my child be prompt in returning the audio book.

_____ For health reasons, my child has his/her own ear buds.

_____ I am sending 2 (or more) AAA batteries to help defray the high use of batteries for the Playaways. (Each Playaway will be sent home with a spare battery.)

Signed: _____
                            Parent or Guardian

Child: _____

Date: _____

Teacher: _____

Dewey Bingo

Objectives: To become familiar with the ten Dewey categories. To know that specific topics have specific numbers in the Dewey decimal system

Grades: 3–5

Materials:

- bingo cards

- beans to use for covers

- extra book coupon or other prize

- Dewey bookmarks, optional, available for purchase from www.highsmith.com and other suppliers

Prepare in Advance:

1. Generate and print 25 bingo cards using the Bingo Generator at www.teach-nology.com/web_tools/materials/bingo/5. Mount each card on construction paper. See the sample on page 17.

2. Place enough beans or counters into 25 small cups for students to use as covers.

3. Prepare a master list so you will know which books have been called.

4. Cut up a duplicate of the master list to use as strips for calling out the titles.

Hints for generating the cards:

1. It appears that the amount of text that fits in each box is limited to a small window. However, keep typing and the line of type will move so you can type an entire title.

2. Don't use a free space. If you do, the program randomly assigns the free space, giving some children a better advantage than others. Instead, use 25 Dewey subjects.

3. Be sure to print the card you see before hitting "shuffle words."

4. The card will print without the letters B. I. N. G. O. at the top. It won't matter in this version of the game because the announced title could be in any of the five columns.

5. Cut out the cards, glue to construction paper, and laminate.

Activity Directions:

1. Before the game, give each child a Dewey bookmark (which they can keep if you have enough). Draw out a card and read it. Unlike Bingo, the matching number could be anywhere on the card, not just in one column. Play leisurely to give children a chance to look at their cards. After each one, ask what category that is. For example, Reptiles 597.9 would be in the 500s, Natural Science. Play for about 15 minutes or until you get eight winners, whichever comes first.

2. Give the winners the coupon below to turn in when they check out their extra book. If they have overdue books and can't check out, they can give the book coupon to a friend—but it must be redeemed in this class.

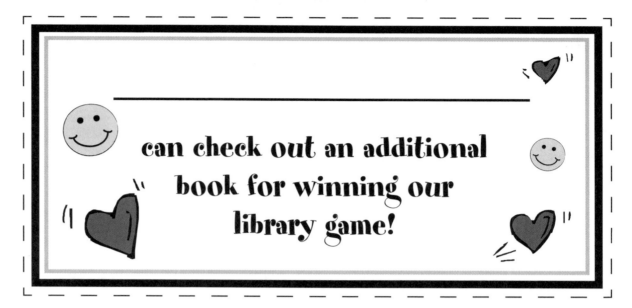

can check out an additional book for winning our library game!

Keep Reluctant Readers Reading

I've tried a number of things for those students who forget to return their books. Having them read magazines or work on activity sheets caused circulation to drop because reluctant readers discovered if they "forgot" their books, they didn't have to get another, but could have "fun" instead. Now I have them check out one book (normally they get two) and we save it in boxes behind the counter. If they come back any time the next day, they can claim the book without waiting in the check out line.

Use three plastic tubs or boxes with signs clipped to the front with clothes pins. You can use the sign patterns on pages 18 and 19. If today is Wednesday, the signs clipped to the three boxes will say Monday, Tuesday, and Wednesday. You will check in and shelve the unclaimed books that were checked out on Monday. Keep the Tuesday books handy to be claimed all day Wednesday. Fill the Wednesday box with books checked out by today's forgetful students, each of which has their name on a sticky note (filled out by the child).

Each morning, empty the "oldest" box, clip today's sign on it and move it to the right end of the group of three.

Bingo Card

597.9 Reptiles	394.2 Holidays	398.2 Folk and Fairy Tales	796.332 Football	597.8 Frogs
629.4 Space Travel	636.1 Horses	133.1 Ghost Sightings	031 Guiness Book of World Records	629.133 Airplanes
793.8 Magic	551.2 Volcanoes	599.75 Big Cats	743 Drawing	940.54 World War II
811 Poetry	608 Inventions	636.7 Dogs	567.9 Dinosaurs	641.5 Cookbooks
932 Ancient Egypt	398.8 Transportation	220.9 Bible Stories	292 Mythology	468 Spanish

Checked Out Monday

Checked Out Tuesday

Checked Out Wednesday

Checked Out Thursday

Checked Out Friday

Book Fair Options

Librarians are programmed to find ways to get books into the hands of their students, hoping that possession is a key factor in reading. Book Fairs are a great way to get permanent possession of books into the hands and homes of students, increasing the likelihood that those books will be read. There are a number of ways to host a fair.

LOCAL CHAIN BOOKSTORE

The easiest is to arrange for your local chain bookstore to advertise a day that is your school's Book Fair. On that day (and night), a percentage of all books sales goes to your school.

Advantages

- Your school earns money on the sales not only of your students and their parents, but of anyone who makes a purchase that day/night.

- Your fair's selection includes the entire store: children's and adult books.

- No set-up or take-down is needed.

- There is no problem with re-orders.

- Library lessons can continue since the library doesn't become the site of the fair.

Disadvantages

- Because the fair isn't at school, many students will not attend.

- Students don't make a preview wish list that helps parents narrow the field.

- The fair lasts only one day.

- The store location may not be convenient to your school.

- The library is not the site, so the library is not the focus of the enthusiasm on the part of shoppers.

INDEPENDENT BOOKSTORE OR BOOK JOBBER

In this day of mammoth national chains, it is symbiotic for the school libraries to support their independent booksellers when they can. One way is to have an independent book store stock your book fair.

Advantages

- The selection can be custom tailored to your students and their interests.

- Restocks are often quicker because the store is close to your school.

- You can often handpick your book fair.

- Goodwill is built between you and your independent bookstore—both of which make it their mission to satisfy the reading needs of the locals.

- They will often assist with unpacking and packing your fair.

- Service is more personal.

Disadvantages

- Often cannot offer the profit margin of the national book fair company.

- Usually there are no free books or other sales incentives.

- Must supply your own tables.

- Book fair displays are usually flat on tables, which can be more difficult for children to see.

- You may be expected to inventory books before and after the fair, or if the company does so, you will be expected to pay for any that "walk" during your fair.

NATIONAL BOOK FAIR COMPANY

Over the years, Scholastic Book Fairs has bought out the other national book fair companies. It has tried to streamline the entire process, providing training, a preview DVD, forms, online reorders, and online reporting forms.

Advantages

- The fair is delivered in rolling book cases that display the books facing front.

- Training provides you and/or your chair with decorating ideas, how to set-up and operate your fair, etc.

- A preview video introduces students to a number of authors and titles that will be in their book fair and generates enthusiasm.

- Take home flyer showing books, hall and exterior posters advertising sale, and letters, clip art and other forms are provided.

- Large selection, often at lower prices than chains or bookstores.

- Size of company allows for a larger percentage of profits, and often includes allowance for book prizes to distribute during fair as well as some free books for the library.

- Can take profit in cash, or double the profit to choose books and instructional materials from their catalog.

- Will often provide cash register and credit card machine.

- You are not expected to inventory the books.

- Company will absorb a small number of losses due to books that walk.

Disadvantages

Numerous fairs are booked simultaneously, so service may suffer depending on time of your fair.

- Selection is prepackaged, though you can request that certain packages be added or deleted (Spanish titles, adult books, YA books).

- Reorders are often a problem because books are shipped from centralized warehouses which may not be close to your school.

- Service may be less personal since sales force has a large territory.

- Send a number of gift items which detract from book sales, or must be stored if you decide not to display.

When making your choice, you have to weigh a number of factors. Here are some questions to ask yourself and/or your book fair representative:

How much do you want to be involved in the fair itself?

How long will the fair run?

How much help do you have?

How experienced are you with book fairs?

Can you afford to take less profit to have personalized stock and service?

Does your supplier ask you to inventory books in and out of your fair and pay for the difference?

Can you request special orders?

How many fairs are they doing concurrently with yours?

How often do they restock your fair and how?

What percentage of sales do they give you?

Will they provide a cashier (usually he/she is "paid" by shaving off some of your percentage)?

What is the price range of the books? Are any items available for less than $2.00 if that is needed for your students?

Is there a discount for teachers? Do you want to provide this perk or do you expect teachers to make the same contribution to the library as the students?

Genre Soccer

Objectives: To identify whether a book is nonfiction. To identify whether a book is fiction. For upper grades: If it is fiction, to identify if it is realistic fiction or fantasy.

Grades: K–2, 3–5

Materials:

- pencils

- stack of 10 age-appropriate books (page 25)

- some nonfiction, some realistic fiction, and some fantasy books

- copy of worksheet for each child or each pair

Prepare in Advance:

1. Sharpen pencils.

2. Select books.

3. Duplicate worksheets.

Activity Directions:

1. Explain to students the difference between the books and give them examples. Fiction is From Imagination (fiction begins with f and i from those two words), nonfiction is NOT From Imagination—it is true. These two are opposites and they are often kept on opposite sides of a library.

2. Explain that in fiction, the author can imagine two main kinds of books. One kind could possibly happen in real life—it's called REAListic fiction. The other kind is fantasy—it couldn't possibly happen because of the unrealistic things the characters do, like time travel or flying people, or because the characters don't occur in real life, like talking animals or unicorns, ogres, and fairies.

3. As a warm-up, ask students to think of a fantasy story they have heard about or read. Allow a couple of minutes for each person to think of one. Tell them that you will go to each person. If they can think of one without repeating, they score a point for their class. If they are incorrect or can't think of one, you score a point. Proceed to each child, elaborating where necessary and keeping score.

4. Repeat the same procedure with realistic fiction.

5. Explain the Genre Soccer score sheet on page 25. Next, hold up the book, giving the summary if necessary and have everyone circle the genre they think it is. Check after each one and have them give themselves a tally mark at the bottom if they guess correctly. For example, hold up Geronimo Stilton's *Mona Mousa Code* and tell students that all the mice work for a newspaper in New Mouse City and are involved in a variety of adventures together. Primary students circle fiction or nonfiction. Older readers look across row one.

First, they should decide if this book is a fiction or nonfiction book. If it is fiction, is it realistic or fantasy? Everyone circles, then ask the class to say the answer and everyone checks. If a child has the correct answer, she scores a tally mark in the score box at the bottom of the page.

To Get a Book or Not To Get a Book—That Is the Question

Does it pain you when a child wants to leave the library without a book? What can be done? Do you force the child to take a book, knowing that if you hid $10 in the book, it would still be there when the book was returned?

My experience is that students refuse to choose books for three reasons:

1. They can't find a book, translated as "There aren't any good books in this library."

2. Their teachers understandably want them to get a book on their low reading level, embarrassing them in front of peers.

3. If they don't get a book, they can evade book-related activities.

Recently I was in my local book store with a discount coupon and a generous gift card. Unlike some of my students, I was ready, able and willing to get a book. Like my students, I couldn't think of any of the authors or titles of books that I had read reviews of or series I wanted to continue. I wandered the aisles, hoping a book would jump out at me—exactly the strategy many of my students use. What helped me finally purchase books? Book displays, lists of best sellers, staff recommendations, and a big sale table.

How can we translate that for our libraries? Book displays are a challenge for me, not because I can't or don't want to do them, but because the first classes wipe them out and then I don't have time to restock them.

Book Star Team Displays

One solution is to have a Book Star Team composed of students or parent volunteers. It's helpful if the team is a mix of reading levels and that you have one at every grade level. When they come to the library for their own check out, they can pull 3 or 4 extra books that appeal to them and put them into the display. Or you can make it a policy that students who finish checking out early can choose books for the display. What if those who say they don't or can't get books become the selectors? Then they are still looking at books and feel valued rather than frustrated. They might even discover a book they want.

Low Reading Level Blues

I am one who does not believe in putting color-coded reading level labels on the book spines. We put them on a white sticker on the back of the book where students or teachers can see them, but not peers. Arrange with the teacher for the child to check out an appropriate lower level book while on a pass—and not with their class. Perhaps they can leave the book with you and pick it up just before dismissal while carrying his/her backpack so it can be stashed.

Name _____ Teacher_____

 **Genre Soccer**

Score a goal for each one you get correct!

Nonfiction	Fiction	
1. nonfiction	realistic fiction	fantasy
2. nonfiction	realistic fiction	fantasy
3. nonfiction	realistic fiction	fantasy
4. nonfiction	realistic fiction	fantasy
5. nonfiction	realistic fiction	fantasy
6. nonfiction	realistic fiction	fantasy
7. nonfiction	realistic fiction	fantasy
8. nonfiction	realistic fiction	fantasy
9. nonfiction	realistic fiction	fantasy
10. nonfiction	realistic fiction	fantasy

Score Box

Add a hatch mark for every correct answer.

Nonfiction Features Scavenger Hunt

Objectives: To identify and locate a variety of useful nonfiction text features appropriate to each grade level.

Grades: K–2, 3–5

Materials:

- pencils

- copies of the appropriate scavenger hunt for the grade

- a nonfiction book for each student to use that includes the text features sought in the scavenger hunt. I use *A Pet for Every Person* (UpstartBooks, 2007) because it is colorful, appealing, and contains all the features included on the worksheet. It also comes with small matching versions that can be used with the children. I can attest that they are very durable!

- An optional method would be to give each child a different nonfiction book. After they find and record their answer, they check to see if they and their partner agree with the choices each made. This gives them twice the practice.

- Find a book to use as the example to show what each part looks like—either before or after the answer.

Prepare in Advance:

1. Gather the books you will use.

2. Duplicate the appropriate grade level scavenger hunt sheets.

3. Select the example book you will use with students.

Back in the Day

A student was at the computer looking for information on Dr. Martin Luther King, Jr. He raised his hand and said, "My daddy said when he was a little boy, Dr. King was still alive. Could that really be true?"

I asked how old his dad was and said that, yes, it was true. The student asked me if I was a little baby when Dr. King died and I honestly replied, "No, I was in college." The student paused and then asked, "Did YOUR daddy own slaves?"

—Katie Sessler, Librarian
Jackson MS Library, Grand Prairie, TX

Activity Directions:

1. Before you show the students, tell them that when they are done looking at the example book, you will give them each a scavenger hunt sheet, a pencil, and a nonfiction book. They will have _____ minutes to look through the book to find as many of the features as they can.

2. To review the parts of a book, show students in your big book *A Pet for Every Person* (or the example nonfiction book you chose) the nonfiction features they are going to be searching for.

3. Go through the example book, demonstrating and talking about the purposes and uses of the various text features.

4. Distribute the pencils, scavenger sheets, and nonfiction books. Tell students to do the ones they are familiar with first. At the end of _____ minutes, they will have to stop and check. They only have to write the page number on which that information is found. For example, the title can be found on the title page (page 1). Don't write the title; write a 1 in the box. If there is more than one feature, they only write one page number.

5. Give students the allocated amount of time, circulating to see if you can help students who are stuck. Sometimes a reminder about the meaning of the word is all that is needed to jog their ability to locate the feature.

6. After time is up, check their work orally. If you all have the same book, the answers will be the same. If books are different, partners check each other's work.

Free and Fantastic

Most of us have had the experience of doing something simple for students that turns out to be a big hit. Mitzi Cross, librarian at a neighboring school in my district, was asked for a bookmark. She is librarian at a new school and had no bookmarks. However, she did have about 40 feet of backing tape from the label covers she was affixing to new books, so she cut off a length and gave it to the student. The child was so delighted with the novelty of the bookmark that she told her friends and Mitzi was besieged with requests for the shiny white bookmarks!

I had a similar experience where I had little budget for an activity to reward students who had completed the requirements for our school's reading club. So I invited the qualifying students to a picnic we called "Books on the Beach." They could bring a beach towel, their lunch, and sunglasses. We moved the tables out of the way and students spread their towels by their friends for lunch. The library provided the boom box. Students brought in their favorite CDs and I played them throughout the picnic. I gave each child door prizes and gave each child a die cut bookmark to which I attached a label that said, "I earned a trip to 'Books on the Beach'!" It was so memorable they wanted it to be an annual event, and it cost me nothing.

Name _____

Nonfiction Features Scavenger Hunt
Grades K–1

Find the feature, and write the page number in the box.

1. bibliography	6. index
2. caption	7. label
3. copyright page	8. map
4. dedication page	9. table of contents
5. glossary	10. title page

Name _____

Nonfiction Features Scavenger Hunt

Grades 2–3

Find the feature, and write the page number in the box.

1. bibliography	8. graph
2. caption	9. index
3. chart	10. label
4. copyright page	11. map
5. dedication page	12. table of contents
6. diagram	13. time line
7. glossary	14. title page

Name _____

Nonfiction Features Scavenger Hunt

Grades 4–5

Find the feature, and write the page number in the box.

1. appendix	11. glossary
2. bibliography	12. graph
3. caption	13. index
4. chart	14. label
5. table	15. map
6. comparison	16. sidebar
7. copyright page	17. summary or blurb
8. cutaway	18. table of contents
9. dedication page	19. time line
10. diagram	20. title page

Answer Key for Grades K–1:

1. bibliography	22	6. index	24
2. caption	8, 10, 16	7. label	9, 11, 16, 18, 20
3. copyright page	2	8. map	18
4. dedication page	2	9. table of contents	3
5. glossary	23	10. title page	1

Answer Key for Grades 2–3:

1. bibliography	22	8. graph	4
2. caption	8, 10, 16	9. index	24
3. chart	6, 19	10. label	9, 11, 16, 18, 20
4. copyright page	2	11. map	18
5. dedication page	2	12. table of contents	3
6. diagram	11, 16	13. time line	9
7. glossary	23	14. title page	1

Answer Key for Grades 4–5: (page numbers are for *A Pet for Every Person**)

1. appendix	21	11. glossary	23
2. bibliography	22	12. graph	4
3. caption	8, 10, 16	13. index	24
4. chart	6, 19	14. label	9, 11, 16, 18, 20
5. table	9, 20	15. map	18
6. comparison	11, 20	16. sidebar	11
7. copyright page	2	17. summary or blurb	Back cover
8. cutaway	16	18. table of contents	3
9. dedication page	2	19. time line	9
10. diagram	11, 16	20. title page	1

*NOTE: On page 19, the twenty-fifth name is a misprint. It should be Sheba. You can ask students in the older grades to locate the misprint as a bonus question.

Get to Know George

Objectives: Learn some little-known information about the Father of Our Country.

Grades: 3–5

Materials:

- *George Washington's Teeth*
- George Washington tag game

Prepare in Advance:

1. Reproduce and cut up tag card games. If you will play with multiple classes, you may want to make extras to replace the first set when it becomes dog-eared and dirty.

2. Find *George Washington's Teeth*.

Activity Directions:

1. We celebrate George Washington's birthday (February 22, 1732) this month, as well as the facts that he was the first American president and was so involved in the founding and beginning growth of our nation. Explain that the students are going to learn some amazing facts about the pain with which Washington lived and how he continued to achieve despite it.

2. Show students the book and tell them that you are going to be reading the book aloud to them in a few minutes. However, before you read, you wanted to see how much they know about the topic. Tell them you will read a statement and they are to thumbs up for true, thumbs down for false. (Thumbs sideways if they don't know.)

3. Read the following statements. Do not reveal whether they are true. Students will discover their veracity when they read the book.

    Thumbs up, thumbs down:

    1. There are no pictures of George Washington smiling. (T)

    2. There were no dentists in George Washington's time. (F)

    3. GW's lost a lot of teeth as an adult. (T)

    4. GW lost his teeth because they were black and rotten. (T)

    5. GW and his army were fighting the French. (F)

    6. GW used wooden teeth when he lost his real teeth. (F)

7. George used his old teeth and some plaster to make dentures. (T)

8. George's wife was named Polly. (F) Martha

9. George died early (age 67) due in part to an infection of old root fragments. (T)

10. His last dentures were made from hippo teeth. (T)

4. Read the book, stopping when students hear confirmation about the statements above. After, play the George Washington Tag Game. This game has been slightly modified from one of hundreds of literature activities Suzy Red has on her Web site (www.suzyred.com), as well as hundreds more for science, social studies, math, and many other topics.

5. To play George Washington Tag Game: Each student gets a card with an answer and a question. The student with question Card #1 asks the question. The student with the answer to that question stands, reads the answer, and asks his question. The answer to the last question is on Card #1. For the original game, visit suzyred.com/2004washingtoncardgame.pdf. You can also order a number of her activity books at this site.

Resources:

The George Washington You Never Knew by James Lincoln Collier. Children's Press, 2003.

George Washington's Teeth by Deborah Chandra and Madeleine Comora. Farrar, Straus and Giroux, 2003.

Take the Lead, George Washington by Judith St. George. Philomel Books, 2005.

Where Washington Walked by Raymond Bial. Walker & Co., 2004.

READ THIS LAST:

Answer: He wrote journals.

Q: Where was George Washington born?

A: On a farm in Virginia

Q: In what year was George Washington born?

A: 1732

Q: Who was George Washington afraid would laugh at him because of his teeth?

A: The British

Q: In what year was George Washington's first tooth extracted?

A: 1756

Q: How old was George Washington when his first tooth was extracted?

A: 24 years old

Q: What soft food did George Washington eat?

A: The rubbery lining of the stomach of a cow or sheep that was preserved in vinegar

Q: In which war was Washington elected commander-in-chief of the Continental army?

A: Revolutionary War

Q: In the portrait of George Washington at age 44, how can you tell he had bad teeth?

A: He has a scar on his left cheek caused by a rotten tooth.

Q: What did George do with his teeth when they fell out?

George Washington's Teeth Card Tag

A: He saved them.

Q: How were his saved teeth helpful?

A: They were used as models for his false teeth.

Q: What was his last set of false teeth made from?

A: hippo teeth

Q: What caused George Washington to have frequent fevers and infections?

A: old root fragments and rotting teeth

Q: What caused his deafness?

A: the unnatural motion of his lower jaw when he wore his lower dentures

Q: What was the main reason George wore dentures?

A: for his appearance

Q: How many of his own teeth did George have when he was elected president?

A: two

Q: In what year did George become president?

A: 1789

Q: What was the name of George Washington's house?

A: Mount Vernon

Q: What could George not do while wearing his dentures?

George Washington's Teeth Card Tag

A: chew

Q: How did the dentures make George act?

A: grumpy

Q: What stained his dentures?

A: wine

Q: It's not true that George Washington's teeth were made from what?

A: wood

Q: To make him look better in portraits, what did they pad his lips and cheeks with?

A: cotton

Q: What character trait did George learn from his dental problems?

A: perseverance (He didn't give up even though he was in pain.)

Q: How do we know so much about George's teeth?

George Washington's Teeth Card Tag Answer Sheet

READ THIS LAST: A: He wrote journals

Q: Where was George Washington born?

A: On a farm in Virginia

Q: In what year was George Washington born?

A: 1732

Q: Who was George Washington afraid would laugh at him because of his teeth?

A: The British

Q: In what year was George Washington's first tooth extracted?

A: 1756

Q: How old was George Washington when his first tooth was extracted?

A: 24 years old

Q: What soft food did George Washington eat?

A: The rubbery lining of the stomach of a cow or sheep that was preserved in vinegar

Q: In which war was Washington elected commander-in-chief of the Continental army?

A: Revolutionary War

Q: In the portrait of George Washington at age 44, how can you tell he had bad teeth?

A: He has a scar on his left cheek caused by a rotten tooth.

Q: What did George do with his teeth when they fell out?

A: He saved them.

Q: How were his saved teeth helpful?

A: They were used as models for his false teeth.

Q: What was his last set of false teeth made from?

A: hippo teeth

Q: What caused George Washington to have frequent fevers and infections?

A: old root fragments and rotting teeth

Q: What caused his deafness?

A: the unnatural motion of his lower jaw when he wore his lower dentures

Q: What was the main reason George wore dentures?

A: for his appearance

Q: How many of his own teeth did George have when he was elected president?

A: two

Q: In what year did George become president?

A: 1789

Q: What was the name of George Washington's house?

A: Mount Vernon

Q: What could George not do while wearing his dentures?

A: chew

Q: How did the dentures make George act?

A: grumpy

Q: What stained his dentures?

A: wine

Q: It's not true that George Washington's teeth were made from what?

A: wood

Q: To make him look better in portraits, what did they pad his lips and cheeks with?

A: cotton

Q: What character trait did George learn from his dental problems?

A: perseverance (He didn't give up even though he was in pain.)

Q: How do we know so much about George's teeth?

NOTE: Circle back to first question.

My Brother Martin

Objectives: To relate to Dr. Martin Luther King, Jr. by learning about his childhood. To compare the life of a famous person to one's own to see that ordinary people can do extraordinary things.

Grades: K–2, 3–5

Materials:

*   *My Brother Martin*

*   transparency of "Maybe Some Day..." for grades 3–5 (page 41)

Prepare in Advance:

1. Make a transparency and a student reproducible.

2. Locate and become familiar with the book.

You Can Never Know Too Much

When a junior high student checked out all the Martin Luther King, Jr. books in my library for a research project, she also had one on Martin Luther. When I pointed out that Martin Luther and Martin Luther King were not the same person, she said, "Oh, I know but I thought it wouldn't hurt to know a little about his father, too."

—Bonnie Rice, Librarian
La Vernia Junior High, TX

Activity Directions:

1. Ask students what they know about Martin Luther King, Jr. Jot down what they mention. Then ask what they think he was like as a child and jot that down in a second column.

2. Read *My Brother Martin* to students. This biography was written by Martin's sister and she reveals details that may surprise students. My students figured that Martin had his dream while in grade school and that he was very peaceful as a child. They were delighted to discover he was a lot like them.

3. For K–2: Go back to the children's list from step 1 and have them tell you which statements turned out to be accurate. What would they add now that they've heard the book? Can they think of any way in which they are like Martin Luther King? Have them turn to the person next to them to talk about how they are alike. Then ask the group what they decided.

4. For 3–5: Help the students to make the point that famous adults usually don't know they are going to be famous when they are children, just as they don't know if they will be. But they do have some qualities, ideas, values, and hopes as children that will be an important part of who they are in the future. Show students the transparent version of "Maybe Some Day..." sheet. Have students think about each statement. Then ask if students would like to share with another student.

5. Instead of asking fourth and fifth graders to share, you may feel a need to protect them from being teased or feeling vulnerable by asking them, "What qualities do students have today that will help others in the future?" They can give examples if desired (sense of humor, kindness, willingness to share, good ideas, etc.).

Resources (These include information about Martin's childhood):

Free at Last! The Story of Martin Luther King, Jr. by Angela Bull. DK Publishing, 2000.

A Lesson for Martin Luther King, Jr. by Denise Lewis Patrick. Aladdin, 2003.

Martin Luther King, Jr.: Champion of Civil Rights by Edith Hope Fine. Enslow Elementary, 2006.

My Brother Martin: A Sister Remembers Growing Up with the Rev. Dr. Martin Luther King, Jr. by Christine King Farris. Simon & Schuster Books for Young Readers, 2003.

A Picture Book of Martin Luther King, Jr. by David A. Adler. Holiday House, 1989.

Maybe Some Day...

1. A quality I am proud of is:

2. My family would tell you I am good at:

3. What makes me a good friend is that I:

4. Something I think I would be good at is:

5. People would be surprised to know that I:

Love Your Library Month

"A Year of Reading: Two Teachers Who Read. A Lot." is the blog of Franki and Mary Lee. On it they have listed books about books and reading. Share any of these during this month, or make a display. Franki and Mary Lee also invited readers to submit the names of "cool" teachers in literature and the titles of the books in which they appear. Look for "100 Cool Teachers in Children's Literature" at <u>readingyear.blogspot.com/2007/01/master-list-books-about-books-and.html</u>.

Books about Books and Reading

<u>Picture Books</u>

How a Book is Made by Aliki

Read Anything Good Lately? by Susan Allen and Jane Lindaman

Souper Chicken by Mary Jane and Herm Auch

The Best Place to Read by Debbie Bertram and Susan Bloom

The Best Time to Read by Debbie Bertram and Susan Bloom

Wolf by Becky Bloom

The Day Eddie Met the Author by Louise Borden

Across a Dark and Wild Sea by Don Brown

But Excuse Me That is my Book by Lauren Child

Book! by Kristine O'Connell George

Check it Out! The Book About Libraries by Gail Gibbons

The Incredible Book Eating Boy by Oliver Jeffers

Library Lion by Michelle Knudsen

Jake's 100th Day of School by Lester Laminack

Book by George Ella Lyon

Santa's Book of Names by David McPhail

Edward and the Pirates by David McPhail

Edward in the Jungle by David McPhail

Tomás and the Library Lady by Pat Mora

Amelia Hits the Road by Marissa Moss

The Girl Who Hated Books by Manjusha Pawagi

Aunt Chip and the Great Triple Creek Dam Affair by Patricia Polacco

Thank You, Mr. Falker by Patricia Polacco

Reading Grows by Ellen Senisi

Wild About Books by Judy Sierra

The Hard Times Jar by Ethel Footman Smothers

From Pictures to Words: A Book About Making a Book by Janet Stevens

The Library by Sarah Stewart

Library Lil by Suzanne Williams

The Old Woman Who Loved to Read by John Winch

The Librarian of Basra by Jeanette Winter

Chapter Books

Magic by the Book by Nina Berenstein

Matilda by Roald Dahl

Seven Day Magic by Edward Eager

Inkheart by Cornelia Funke

The Big Green Book by Robert Graves

Fly By Night by Francis Hardinge

The Book of Story Beginnings by Kristin Kladstrup

Looking Back: A Book of Memories by Lois Lowry

Summer Reading is Killing Me by Jon Scieszka

At the Sign of the Star by Katherine Sturtevant

The Great Good Thing by Roderick Townley

Poetry

Good Books, Good Times by Lee Bennett Hopkins

The Bookworm's Feast by J. Patrick Lewis

Please Bury Me in the Library by J. Patrick Lewis

Substitute Groundhog Reader's Theater

Objectives: To enjoy a shared reading and to perform a story from a reader's script.

Grades: K–2, 3–5

Materials:

- Reader's Theater scripts, marked for each reader with extras for the librarian and teacher if she stays (pages 46–49)

- If this performance is done in a partnership, you will need puppets or stuffed animals for the younger performers. You will need a groundhog, mole, bear, eagle, squirrel, and armadillo. Or, use the Character Patterns on pages 50–53 to enlarge and put on tongue depressors to use as stick puppets instead.

Alter Ego

For several years, I was a librarian at two elementary libraries. I traveled to one school for two days each week and the other for three. When I was at one school library, the library aide would work at the other school. One day after school, a young student brought his mother into the library. Before he checked out his library book, he looked at me and informed his mother in a loud whisper, "She's the real librarian, the other lady is a fake."

—Kay Davis Spencer, Librarian
Wedgewood Elementary, Clear Creek ISD, TX

Background Information:

Folk wisdom says that if the groundhog sees its shadow on February 2, winter will last six weeks longer. No shadow means spring is on its way. Because February 2 is the middle of winter, early American farmers had a saying, "Groundhog Day, half your hay." Farmers who had less than half their hay left by then would have animals going hungry before the spring grass came in.

To find out the official American groundhog verdict, go to the Web site of America's expert, Punxatawney Phil who lives on Gobbler's Knob in Pennsylvania. A venerable succession of chubby, sleepy Punxatawney Phils have been predicting the end of winter since 1886 (<u>www. goundhog.org</u>). Read about all the past predictions and the current celebratory activities.

Prepare in Advance:

1. To help the audience know which animal is speaking, use the Character Patterns on pages 50–53. You can make them into transparencies and project them onto sheets of fun foam to trace, or can simply duplicate them on cardstock. Make headbands or attach them to wooden sticks that students hold up like stop signs while reading their lines.

2. Duplicate the appropriate number of scripts, including one for yourself and one for the teacher if she stays for the lesson.

3. Highlight the character in the list of parts, and then in the script. Be sure to apprise the audience that the voice of Groundhog may change, but there is only one Groundhog in this story.

Activity Directions:

1. Locate Punxatawney, PA on a large map of the United States. Locate your school's home on the same map to see how far you are from the site of this national event. (For grades 3–5, explain how to use the scale of miles to figure the distance.)

2. *Substitute Groundhog* tells the tale of what might happen if Groundhog was sick for Groundhog Day and had to recruit a substitute. Before performing the readers' theater for *Substitute Groundhog,* read the book aloud. Students will benefit from hearing your expression and pacing, especially to bring out the humor in the story.

3. To choose parts, you can have the teacher decide. Or, you can number the chairs students sit in and randomly select numbers from a jar (use bingo numbers to save time); or choose all animals except Groundhog and let the audience participate by chorally reading his part (you will need highlighted scripts for students to share).

4. Distribute the scripts. Because Groundhog has the largest part in this script, you might want to appoint several Groundhog readers. If you want to split his part, look for "Groundhog 2" to start the second reader. Each will have half the lines. To include one more reader, divide Groundhog's lines into thirds. Look for "Groundhog B" and "Groundhog C".

Resources:

The Groundhog Day Book of Facts and Fun by Wendie Old. Albert Whitman, 2004.

Groundhogs: Woodchucks, Marmots, and Whistle Pigs by Adele D. Richardson. Bridgestone Books, 2003.

Little Marmots by Anne Royer. Gareth Stevens, 2005.

Substitute Groundhog by Pat Miller. Albert Whitman, 2006.

Substitute Groundhog Reader's Theater

by Pat Miller

Based on the book published by Albert Whitman, 2006.

> **Narrators 1, 2, 3, 4, 5, 6**
>
> **Dr. Owl   Groundhog [Groundhog 2] / [Groundhog B, Groundhog C]**
>
> **Bear   Mole   Eagle   Squirrel   Armadillo   Badger**

Narrator 1:	The day before Groundhog Day, Groundhog woke up sick.
Narrator 2:	His muscles ached and his throat hurt.
Narrator 3:	Groundhog felt so awful he went to see Dr. Owl.
Dr. Owl:	You have a bad case of flu, you do. You need bed rest for two days.
Groundhog:	How many?
Dr. Owl:	Two, two, two.
Narrator 4:	But Groundhog Day is tomorrow!
Narrator 5:	Groundhog couldn't let everyone down because he was too sick to do his job.
Narrator 6:	He tried to think of something.
Groundhog:	What am I going to do?
Narrator 1:	On his way home, Groundhog passed the Hidey Hole Diner.
Narrator 2:	He saw want ads from neighborhood animals tacked to a nearby tree.
Narrator 3:	They gave Groundhog an idea.
Groundhog:	I'll advertise for a substitute groundhog.
Narrator 4:	By 10:00, a line of animals waited to try out.
Groundhog:	*(Sneezing.)* Great! Surely one of you can do Groundhog Day for me.
Narrator 5:	Mole was first.

Groundhog:	You have to go down in my hole. It's pretty dark in there.
Mole:	No problem. My own hole is even darker.
Narrator 6:	Mole got comfortable underground.
Groundhog:	Now come up and look for your shadow!
Narrator 1:	Mole peeked over the edge. His eyes squinted.
Mole:	Is that you, Groundhog?
Groundhog:	This won't work. I need someone who sees well.
Eagle:	I can see from high in the sky!
Narrator 2:	Groundhog looked up and saw Eagle.
Groundhog:	Great! Climb down in the hole and let's practice.
Eagle:	Climb down? Will there be enough room for me to stretch my wings?
Narrator 3:	Eagle stretched his wings VERY wide.
Groundhog [B]:	*(Rubbing throat.)* This won't work. I need someone who sees well and is not bothered by small spaces.
Narrator 4:	Bear stepped up next.
Bear:	My own cave is snug and cozy.
Groundhog:	Great. Climb down and let's practice.
Bear:	This is even more comfy than my own cave.
Groundhog:	Come out and take a look.
Narrator 5:	There was no answer.
Narrator 6:	Groundhog poked his head below ground.
Groundhog [2]:	Bear, come look for your shadow.
Narrator 1:	The only answer was a deep, slow snore.
Narrator 2:	Groundhog was frustrated.
Narrator 3:	The substitute must see well, not be bothered by small spaces, and not fall asleep.

Squirrel:	I can do it, I can do it. Let me try!
Groundhog:	OK. Go down in the hole, come back up, and look for your shadow.
Squirrel:	*(Popping up.)* Wheee! This is fun.
Groundhog:	Did you see your shadow?
Squirrel:	Ooops! I forgot to look.
Narrator 4:	Squirrel dropped down.
Narrator 5:	Squirrel popped up.
Narrator 6:	Down. Up. Down.
Groundhog:	I need someone who will pop up and stay up. Will I ever find a substitute?
Armadillo:	Howdy, Groundhog. How about giving me a chance?
Groundhog [C]:	Who are you?
Armadillo:	I'm Armadillo, up from Texas to visit my cousin, Badger.
Groundhog:	Do you think you can do the job?
Armadillo:	I can. I live in a hole. I like small spaces. I see my shadow just fine. And I will pop up and stay up.
Groundhog:	All right. Let's see how you do.
Narrator 1:	Armadillo climbed below ground.
Narrator 2:	She poked her head up and looked around.
Narrator 3:	Sure enough, she saw her shadow.
Groundhog:	If you see your shadow tomorrow, spring will come early.
Armadillo:	Got it!
Narrator 4:	Groundhog headed to bed.
Narrator 5:	He sipped warm clover soup.
Narrator 6:	He tucked his sore self under the flannel quilt.
Narrator 1:	The next morning, the animals gathered to see what Armadillo would say.

Badger: I served hot chocolate.

Squirrel: I bounced and cheered for Armadillo. You go, girl!

Eagle: I flew high above the trees to see if Armadillo would see her shadow.

Mole: I felt sleepy, but at least I was there. Bear was still in bed.

Armadillo: When I peeked out over the edge of Groundhog's hole, I could see the shadow of my ears. Six more weeks of winter!

Groundhog: Oh no! More winter? I'd feel a lot better if it was spring already.

Armadillo: Spring already? That gives me an idea.

Narrator 2:   Armadillo found Groundhog's suitcase.

Armadillo: Get your gear, Groundhog. You can come home with me to Texas. It is already spring there.

Narrator 3:   Groundhog grabbed his teddy bear and his toothbrush and threw them into his suitcase.

Groundhog: I've always wanted to see Texas. Do you think they have cowboy hats in my size?

Armadillo: Sure as Texas has a Lone Star!

Narrator 4:   Together, they walked through the cold to the bus station.

Narrator 5:   And their shadows followed them all the way there.

Narrator 6:   The End.

Substitute Groundhog Character Patterns

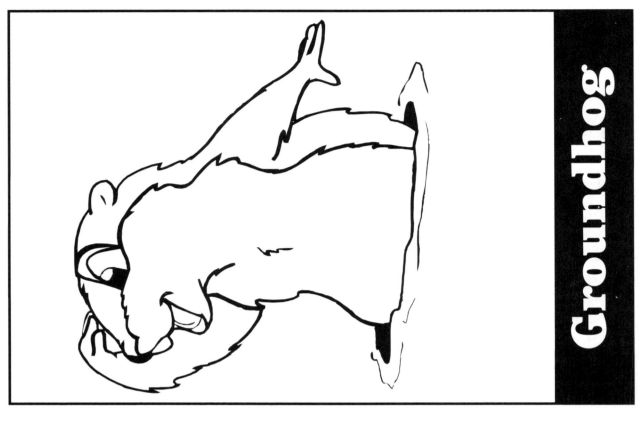

Groundhog

Dr. Owl

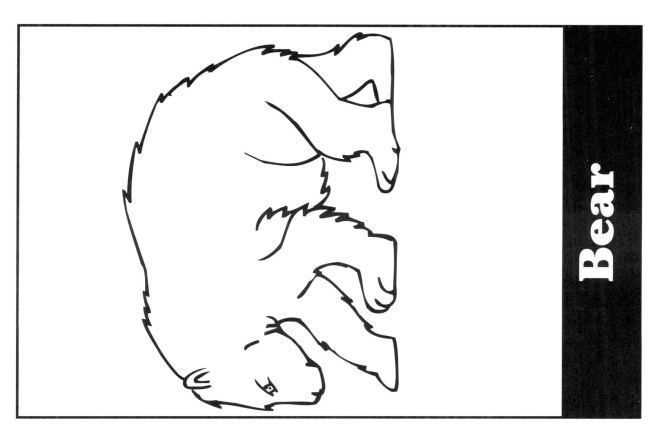

Bear

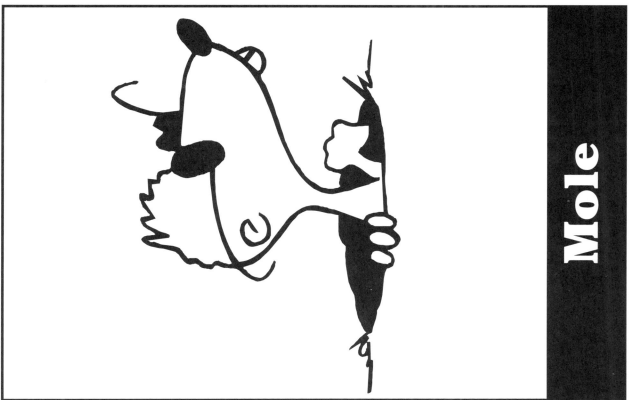

Mole

Eagle

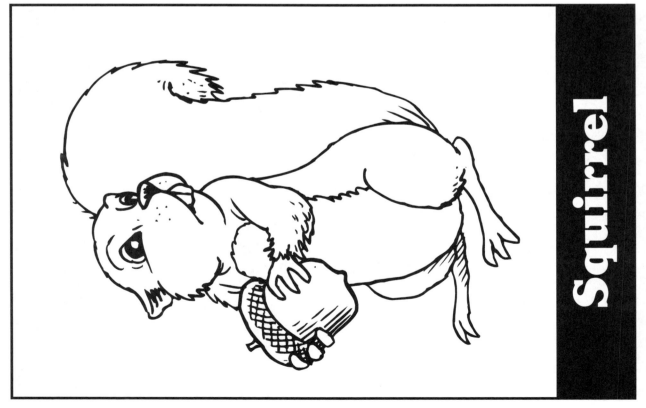

Squirrel

Armadillo

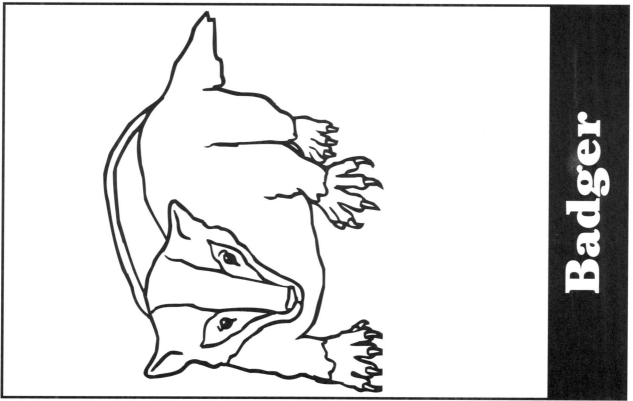

Badger

Writing Reader's Theater Scripts

Objectives: Explore a variety of wordless picture books. Create oral story lines for wordless picture books. Develop a reader's theater script for the wordless book.

Grades: 3–5

Materials:

- a variety of wordless books, enough for every student team with several left over. (See Web sites in resource list.)

- Story Mapping online tool (www.readwritethink.org/materials/storymap/index.html)

- pencils and paper

Prepare in Advance:

1. Gather wordless books.

2. Provide pencils and paper.

3. Set up projector, if possible.

Off the Top of My Head

Preschool students spend lots of time learning their colors. One day, shortly after I had cut and colored my hair, the class was seated in the library, and one student gasped, "Ms. Hunt, you changed your hair! It's green!" We all laughed but I pointed out that my dress was green, and my hair was RED. That was an easy assessment of their color knowledge that day.

—Lisa Hunt, Elementary Library Media Specialist
Moore, OK

Activity Directions:

1. This activity assumes that students are familiar with reader's theater scripts. For practice scripts, stories to use for scripting, and instruction on how to write the scripts, go to www.aaronshep.com/rt/books/ReadersOS.html.

2. Share a wordless book with students, preferably using a projector that will enlarge the pages. Tell students that we will be "reading" silently because each child will be making up their own story in their heads.

3. After seeing the story, reread the story with the students and have students help you tell the story.

4. Give students a wordless book (if possible, let them choose) as a pair. Students are to look through the book once without speaking. Then they can go back and talk together about how they interpret the story.

5. Ask a pair to work on a reader's theater script, using the main characters and one or two narrators to do all the parts that aren't spoken by the characters. You may need to model this process using the book you shared with the class.

6. Students take their book and papers back with them to work on in class. Next library period, they should bring their script back to class to read/perform for students.

Resources:

Weber County Library: Our Recommended Wordless Picture Books
www.weberpl.lib.ut.us/content/booklists/sort/t/31

Wordless Picture Books
picturingbooks.imaginarylands.org/resources/wordless.html

Literary Ideas and Scripts for Young Playwrights by Lisa Kaniut Cobb. Teacher Ideas Press, 2004.

Readers on Stage by Aaron Shepard. Shepard Publications, 2004.
Purchase at www.aaronshep.com/rt/books/ReadersOS.html.

Readers Theater for Building Fluency: Strategies and Scripts for Making the Most of This Highly Effective, Motivating, and Research-Based Approach to Oral Reading by Jo Worthy. Scholastic, 2005.

Readers Theatre for Children: Scripts and Script Development by Mildred Knight Laughlin and Kathy Howard Latrobe. Teacher Ideas Press, 1990.

Tips For Making Your Book Fair a Success

I counted up the number of fairs I've done over my career, and it came to an amazing 43. At various schools, my library has hosted fairs during the school year (usually twice a year), and during summer school. I've used a national book fair company predominantly, but also two local book fair companies. At my first library in a low-income area, we averaged about $1800 in gross sales. At an affluent new school in an area where computer stores hadn't been built yet, the advent of game software in the national book fair boosted our sales to a record $32,000. Along the way, I've learned some tips I would like to pass to you to make your fair easier and more successful.

Infect Students and Teachers with Your Enthusiasm

Book talk some of the books that are coming (get advance copies). Ask your provider to give you some of the "hot" titles for children or ask your students what they want to see in the fair. If you have reluctant readers, ask if there are books that come with objects, like an origami book with paper, or model books that have instructions and the pieces to make the model. Klutz® is a good publisher for these kinds of materials.

If you can get a selection of books in advance, allow teachers to check them out to read to students. Award an entry form for each book they read to students and then have a drawing for free books from returned entries. Students will want to buy books they've heard and liked.

Buy a simple apron from a discount store's craft section and attach a plastic pocket (vinyl is sold by the inch in the same store's fabric center) to the front that is large enough for a picture book. Use paint pen or felt letters to spell, "Coming to the Fair!" Wear the apron for the week before the fair, changing the books often to arouse curiosity as you travel the halls, teach your lessons, etc.

Ask students to make book fair signs from large manila paper that includes the date(s) and times. Choose the best ones to post around school and/or to win the prize you designate. (Can you use some of your profits to pay for Dollar Off coupons?)

Publicize your fair on your school's Web page, marquee, through letters home as well as a wish list. Send home a PR letter that includes a tear form requiring parent signature to return to school to enter the child in a drawing for free books.

If you can get a selection of books in advance, allow teachers to check them out to read to students. Award an entry form (see page 57) for each book they read to students and then have a drawing for free books from returned entries. Students will want to buy books they've heard and liked.

Increase Sales

If your community will support it, provide ways for parents to buy a gift for their child's teacher(s). I've always had teachers make a wish list of books they'd like to receive, including inexpensive and hardcover books. Even more successful was a form that allowed parents to purchase gift certificates for their child's teachers. This gave the teacher a pat on the back, as well as needed funds for books many of the newest young teachers couldn't afford. When we included multiple coupons with our parent letter, parents often gave multiple gifts. These included the music and art teachers, the special education teachers, even the counselor. Create and publicize the gift certificates, sending them home in advance of the fair.

Scholastic will provide a Buy One, Get One Free sale. If the income level of your attendance zone is low, this may be just the fair to allow students to have ownership of books. When I hosted one of these fairs, I displayed only books. The profits for the library are smaller, but the opportunity for book ownership is higher for those with tight budgets.

As much as possible, tailor the fair to the interests of your students. It goes without saying that you will provide a range of reading levels, but include a range of prices as well. Will your community support adult books or preschool books? I've found that every fair I've had supported cookbooks.

Reorders

Use a receipt book that makes two copies. Record the student's name and teacher, the date ordered, title of book, price, and signature of the person who takes the order. Our book has white, yellow, and pink copies. When the book comes in, write DELIVERED and the date and then tear out the yellow copy and tape to the item for delivery. The pink is your copy of what was delivered for an occasion when a parent wonders if the child every received the item. As long as you see a yellow copy, the back order has not come in.

I have read the following book to my students. Please enter my name in the Book Fair drawing for a free book.

Title: _____

Teacher: _____ Grade: _____

Rocks, Writing, and Response

Objectives: To review the rock cycle, become familiar with rock cycle vocabulary, and use that vocabulary to respond to a rock in writing.

Grades: 3–5

Materials:

- a cloth bag

- a book on the rock cycle

- *Everybody Needs a Rock* or *If You Find a Rock*

- a small stone for each child (I use polished stones that are sold by the pound at craft stores.)

- zipped sturdy plastic bags that contain the following: sand, gravel, pebbles, stones, rock (the items get progressively larger)

- a picture of a boulder

- a picture of a mountain

A Month of Reading

For National Reading Month, distribute the reading chart on page 60. Set a deadline and give prizes for completing certain numbers of the events. Duplicate the chart with the verification sheet (page 61) on the back. Mention one or two of the events each week during library class. One of the most memorable ones my students did was a song composed by a student about the book *Shiloh*. She sang it on our televised announcements and was quite a hit. Another was the boy who read a recipe to make double fudge brownies and brought me two. Not original—but my favorite!

Prepare in Advance:

1. Place rocks in a cloth bag so students will choose one without seeing them.

2. Gather books.

3. Prepare to explain the rock cycle, using the materials you have gathered.

Activity Directions:

1. Review the rock cycle and how it contributes to a variety of rocks.

2. Give each student a rock or let them choose, sight unseen, from a small bag.

3. Read *Everybody Needs a Rock* or *If You Find a Rock*. You will see students examining their own rocks as you read. Both books talk about the individuality of rocks and how they can be special to the finder.

4. When you finish, distribute paper and pencils and ask students to respond to the story by agreeing or disagreeing with it, by describing their rock in as much as detail as possible, or by creating a story about their rock. Allow for about 10 minutes or more of writing. Then, ask volunteers to share what they wrote.

5. Divide students into groups of five or six. Have them put all their rocks in the center and look them all over. Can they locate and retrieve their own rock? How?

Resources:

Everybody Needs a Rock by Byrd Baylor. Aladdin 1985.

Experiments on Rocks and the Rock Cycle by Zella Williams. PowerKids Press, 2007.

If You Find a Rock by Peggy Christian. Harcourt, 2000.

The Rock Cycle by Cheryl Jakab. Smart Apple Media, 2008.

The Rock Cycle by Melanie Ostopowich. Weigl Publishers, 2005.

Choral Reading Books

We often read poems, songs, and scripts together. To make them look more professional, I invested in a class set of portfolio binders. These have about 20 page protectors stitched into a vinyl cover. The front cover is made so you can slip in a title page. Each time I have something I want students to read together, I add a copy to the folder and number the pages sequentially.

One day we may be performing Suzy Red's script of *I Stink!*, another we may be singing the words to the groundhog song I made up. All are in the Choral Reading book, with materials for grades K–5. When I put the readers' theater scripts in for the intermediate grades, I highlight the parts as I normally would. Those who receive a script that is not highlighted simply follow along. Those who get a marked script but don't want to be a reader can trade with someone who has a nonreader part.

This idea helps me keep all my scripts, chants, and songs in one place, and students enjoy reading through them after they have performed their own piece. See page 62 for the title page I slip into the front cover of each book.

_____'s Reading Chart

1. Show me your public library card. It should have your name or signature on it.	2. Donate a gently used book to our book drive.	3. Read a realistic fiction book. If you're a boy choose a girl character; if you're a girl, choose a boy character.	4. Grandparents are GRAND. Read a book about a grandparent(s). Are they like yours?	5. Read a scary book. If you gave it a grade for scariness, what would it get?
6. Go to an author's Web site and read it. Read for an interesting fact about him/her.	7. Read a book from a nonfiction section you've never tried.	8. Use reading to follow instructions to make a craft. Show the item to your teacher or librarian.	9. Cook something from reading the recipe. Bring a sample to the library.	10. Memorize a Mother Goose rhyme and tell a friend.
11. Read a Grimm Brothers fairy tale that you've never heard or read before.	12. Use a drawing book to draw (NOT TRACE) something. Show it to your teacher or librarian.	13. Read a book with a color word in the title.	14. Find a book with an irresistible first line. Read the whole book. Was it as good as the first line?	15. Read a book that has won a gold medal. Do you think it deserved the medal?
16. Read a fantasy book where the main characters are animals.	17. Read a magazine article and tell something interesting you learned to a friend.	18. Read a folktale from a country in Asia or Africa. Did you learn something?	19. Set your TV so there is no sound, only captions. Read them for at least 10 minutes.	20. Partner read a picture book where you read a page aloud and then your friend reads the next aloud.
21. Find a poem about something in nature. Read it aloud to your friend or family.	22. Read a nonfiction book to someone younger.	23. Read a book about a holiday or celebration.	24. Follow the directions to perform a science experiment. Show the results.	25. Make up a song about your book's plot. Use the tune to a familiar song. Sing it for your teacher or librarian.

Reading Chart Verification for _____

1. Librarian's signature:
2. Librarian's signature:
3. Title: Main Character's Name:
4. Title: Give one way the grandparent(s) are like or different from yours:
5. Title: Grade Earned:
6. Author: Site: Interesting Fact:
7. Section: Title:
8. Craft: Teacher or Librarian signature:
9. Recipe: Teacher or Librarian signature:
10. Title of rhyme: Family or Friend's signature:
11. Title:
12. Picture of: Teacher or Librarian signature:
13. Title: Fiction or Nonfiction?
14. Title: Yes/No?   First Line:
15. Title: Medal Won: Yes/No?
16. Title:
17. Article Title: Family or Friend's signature:
18. Title: I learned:
19. Title of Program:
20. Title: Family or Friend's signature:
21. Poem title: Family or Friend's signature:
22. Title: Signature of Person Read To:
23. Title:
24. Science Experiment: Signature:
25. Song Title: Signature:

Our Choral Reading Books

Library

(Used with permission.)

No-cost Student Rewards

At one school, we had a schedule where every other Wednesday we had hour-long classes for library, counselor, nurse, and whoever else could be roped into the schedule. Because the makeup of the group changed each time and included random students from each grade, I could not do a regular lesson.

After exhausting my own ideas, I asked my students what they would like to do on "Wonderful Wednesdays" that didn't cost money. They quickly obliged with a list. Their ideas helped me for the rest of the year, but could also be used as rewards for students. Make them the subject of passes that students can earn or events that classes can work towards. Here is what students suggested:

1. Bring in comic books and read with a friend.

2. Cover the tables with sheets or tablecloths and let us read underneath with flashlights (primary).

3. Go outside on pretty days and read to us.

4. Let us pair with the little kids and read books to them.

5. Have a book swap.

6. Do puzzles as teams.

7. Play book charades.

8. Have a longer time to read the magazines.

9. Let us use art supplies to make book jackets or book posters.

10. Read us a book and then show us the movie so we can compare.

11. Make up a book scavenger hunt for us.

12. Let us read with friends from another class with music.

13. We can do book skits.

14. Let us use your puppets to put on shows for each other.

15. Have a dress like a book character contest and give book prizes.

16. Let us make book commercials that you can videotape and put on our school TV.

17. Use the computers to read about our favorite authors and write letters. You send them.

18. Play learning games.

19. More reader's theater scripts.

NOTE: Go to www.librarygames.com/rewards.htm for New Book Passes and other printable student rewards.

Additional Lessons for February

Stretchy Library Lesson Series

Stretchy Library Lessons: Library Skills

"Life Stories" pp. 49–51. Identify the differences between biography, autobiography, and other types of nonfiction books. Use one to create a timeline.

Stretchy Library Lessons: More Library Skills

"Using Reference Tools" pp. 72–82. Gives dog-related task cards for reference stations (dictionary, almanac, encyclopedia, atlas). Next, locate dog breeds and decipher dog idioms using Internet sites.

Stretchy Library Lessons: Multicultural Activities

"Important Contributions" pp. 18–22. Dr. Martin Luther King, Jr. and Mahatma Gandhi were surprisingly similar in their lives and beliefs. Learn more and find out about other contributions from India.

Stretchy Library Lessons: Reading Activities

"Singing Teeth" pp. 20–26. Flannelboard math activity, patterns, and *Ten Little Baby Teeth* song. Instructions for origami tooth pocket and Cause and Effect based on *Andrew's Loose Tooth*.

Stretchy Library Lessons: Research Skills

"The Great Race (Atlas Skills)" pp. 53–59. Everything you need to send students "around the world" in a rousing TV game format.

Stretchy Library Lessons: Seasons & Celebrations

"Library Lover's Month" pp. 61–73. Daily quiz questions for morning announcements, RT script, and character bands for *The Library Dragon*, library logic puzzle, and more.

Collaborative Bridges Series Primary

It's Alive
"Crop to Crunch" pp. 55–69 Apple cycle sequence cards, body measurement math, character and sequence cards for *Little Red Hen*, and a variety of farm to plate activities.

Me, Myself & You
"Friendship" pp. 38–50. RT scripts for *Bubba and Beau, Best Friends* (K–2) and *The Lion and the Mouse* (3–5), friends logic puzzle, make a friend book, learn to settle differences, and more.

Collaborative Bridges Series Intermediate
by Aileen Kirkham

Investigations
"Animal Intelligence: From Intellect to Anatomy", pp. 46–56. Analyze personal intelligence, use brain-to-body ratio to explore animal intelligence, and dissect the human brain's lobes.

People, Places, and Things
"Presidents: Past and Present", pp. 7–22 Interview *The Kid Who Ran for President*, make a presidential bookmark, generate a mini-presidential campaign, and complete the Hall of Fame vs. Wall of Shame chart.

LibrarySparks Correlation for February

If you are a *LibrarySparks* subscriber like me, you may overlook the great lessons in your back issues as you plan for future lessons. To help us both (part of my resolution to be more organized), each month will include references to additional lessons in *LibrarySparks* magazine. If you are not a subscriber, you still have access to the articles with an * on the *LibrarySparks* Web site: www.librarysparks.com. Every issue online and in the magazine includes a calendar with daily books, events, and suggested activities. Most are quick and easy.

February 2004 (Theme: Black History Month)
Crafts: Valentine's Day Story Crafts (K–2, 3–5)
***Crafts:** Additional Valentine's Day Story Crafts (K–2, 3–5)
Curriculum Connections: Black History Month (3–5)
Keep 'Em Reading: *Bud, Not Buddy* Literature Unit (3–5)
Library Lessons: Fiction, Nonfiction & Biography Fun (K–2, 3–5)

Meet the Author: Christopher Paul Curtis (3–5)

Storytime: Noisy Stories (K–2)

Storytime: Two Stories, Two Stories (K–2, 3–5)

February 2005 (Theme: Happy Valentine's Day)

Book Club: A Russian Folktale (1–3)

Curriculum Connections: Valentine's Day (K–2, 3–5)

Keep 'Em Reading: Learning with Lore (K–2, 3–5)

*Keep 'Em Reading: Family Literacy Night (K–2, 3–5)

Library Lessons: Genres (K–2, 3–5)

Meet the Author: Eric Kimmel (K–2, 3–5)

Storytime: Anansi the Spider (K–2)

February 2006 (Theme: Discover Dinosaurs!)

Author Extensions: Studies and Hearts (K–2, 3–5)

Curriculum Connections: Dinosaurs! (K–2, 3–5)

Keep 'Em Reading: What's New, Dinosaur? (3–5)

*Keep 'Em Reading: Curious George Premiere Party (K–2)

*Keep 'Em Reading: Winter Olympics (3–5)

Library Lessons: Note–taking and Outline Skills (3–5)

Meet the Author: Ed Young (K–2, 3–5)

*Meet the Author: Kelly DiPucchio (K–2)

Reader's Theater: *Dinosnores* (K–2)

Storytime: Digging Up Dinosaurs (K–2)

February 2007 (Theme: Free to Fly)	67

Author Extensions: From Dizzy Heights to City Streets (3–5)

Curriculum Connections: The Civil Rights Movement (K–2, 3–5)

In the Spotlight: Sister Tricksters (3–5)

Keep 'Em Reading: The Iditarod: A Race to Learning (3–5)

Library Lessons: Civil Rights (3–5)

*Meet the Author: Deborah Wiles (3–5)

Meet the Illustrator: Christopher Myers (K–2, 3–5)

*Meet the Illustrator: Catherine Stock (K–2, 3–5)

Reader's Theater: *Freedom Summer* (1–3)

Storytime: Shake It All About (K–2)

Bibliography

A

Adler, David A. *A Picture Book of Martin Luther King, Jr.* Holiday House, 1989.

B

Baylor, Byrd. *Everybody Needs a Rock.* Aladdin, 1985.

Bial, Raymond. *Where Washington Walked.* Walker & Co., 2004.

Brett, Jan. *Gingerbread Baby.* Putnam, 1999.

Bull, Angela. *Free at Last! The Story of Martin Luther King, Jr..* DK, 2000.

C

Chandra, Deborah and Madeleine Comora. *George Washington's Teeth.* Farrar, Straus and Giroux, 2003.

Christian, Peggy. *If You Find a Rock.* Harcourt, 2000.

Cobb, Lisa Kaniut. *Literary Ideas and Scripts for Young Playwrights.* Teacher Ideas Press, 2004.

Collier, James Lincoln. *The George Washington You Never Knew.* Children's Press, 2003.

E

Egielski, Richard. *The Gingerbread Boy.* Laura Geringer Books, 1997.

Ernst, Lisa Campbell. *The Gingerbread Girl.* Dutton Children's Books, 2006.

F

Farris, Christine King. *My Brother Martin: A Sister Remembers Growing Up with the Rev. Dr. Martin Luther King, Jr.* Simon & Schuster Books for Young Readers, 2003.

Fine, Edith Hope. *Martin Luther King, Jr.: Champion of Civil Rights.* Enslow Elementary, 2006.

G

Grey, Mini. *Ginger Bear.* Knopf, 2007.

H

Holub, Joan. *The Gingerbread Kid Goes to School.* Grosset & Dunlap, 2002.

J

Jakab, Cheryl. *The Rock Cycle.* Smart Apple Media, 2008.

Jarrell, Randall. *The Gingerbread Rabbit.* HarperCollins, 1996.

L

Laughlin, Mildred Knight. *Readers Theatre for Children: Scripts and Script Development.* Teacher Ideas Press, 1990.

Law, Karina. *The Truth About Hansel and Gretel.* Picture Window Books, 2005.

Leland, Debbie. *The Jalapeño Man.* Wildflower Run Publishing, 2000.

M

McMullan, Kate and Jim McMullan. *I Stink!* Joanna Cotler Books, 2002.

Miller, Pat. *Substitute Groundhog.* Albert Whitman, 2006.

O

Old, Wendie. *The Groundhog Day Book of Facts and Fun.* Albert Whitman, 2004.

Ostopowich, Melanie. *The Rock Cycle.* Weigl Publishers, 2005.

P

Patrick, Denise Lewis. *A Lesson for Martin Luther King, Jr.* Aladdin, 2003.

R

Richardson, Adele D. *Groundhogs: Woodchucks, Marmots, and Whistle Pigs.* Bridgestone Books, 2003.

Royer, Anne. *Little Marmots.* Gareth Stevens, 2005.

S

Sabuda, Robert and Matthew Reinhart. *Pop-Up Handbook: Butterflies.* Hyperion, 2001.

Sabuda, Robert and Matthew Reinhart *Encyclopedia Prehistorica: Dinosaurs.* Candlewick Press, 2005.

Sabuda, Robert. *Alice's Adventures in Wonderland.* Simon & Schuster, 2003.

Sabuda, Robert. *Cookie Count: A Tasty Pop-Up.* Simon & Schuster, 1997.

Sabuda, Robert. *The Movable Mother Goose.* Simon & Schuster, 1999.

Sabuda, Robert. *The Wonderful Wizard of Oz.* Simon & Schuster, 2000.

Shepard, Aaron. *Readers on Stage.* Shepard Publications, 2004.

Sperring, Mark. *The Fairytale Cake.* Scholastic, 2005.

Squires, Janet. *The Gingerbread Cowboy.* Laura Geringer Books, 2006.

St. George, Judith. *Take the Lead, George Washington!* Philomel Books, 2005.

W

Williams, Zella. *Experiments on Rocks and the Rock Cycle.* PowerKids Press, 2007.

Worthy, Jo. *Readers Theater for Building Fluency: Strategies and Scripts for Making the Most of This Highly Effective, Motivating, and Research-Based Approach to Oral Reading.* Scholastic, 2005.